Marcie

Just wanted to
Share this Charming
book with you —

Kathy T.

# A PART

Wendell Berry

*North Point Press*
*San Francisco*
*1980*

Some of the poems in this volume first appeared in the following magazines: *Adena, Apple, Approaches, The Ark, Cold Mountain, Florida Quarterly, The Georgia Review, Green River Review, Handsel, Harper's, Harvard Magazine, Kayak, The Kentucky Poetry Review, Lillabulero, Monk's Pond, The Nation, New England Review, New Salt Creek Reader, North Country, Plainsong, Sequoia, The Small Farm, Southern Poetry Review, The Southern Review, Twigs, The Wandering Foot,* and *Wild Places*. "Another Descent" and "Ronsard's Lament" first appeared in *The Hudson Review*.

A few of these poems appeared in chapbooks published by the following small presses: Best Cellar Press (TO WHAT LISTENS); Cold Mountain Press (THERE IS SINGING AROUND ME); The Deerfield Press (THE GIFT OF GRAVITY); Larkspur Press (THE KENTUCKY RIVER and HORSES); and Sand Dollar (AN EASTWARD LOOK). "Fall" was first published in *Symbolism and Modern Literature, Studies in Honor of Wallace Fowlie* (The Duke University Press).

To my mother,
who gave me books

# Contents

## I

Stay Home  3
To Gary Snyder  4
For the Hog Killing  5
Goods  6
The Adze  7
The Cold Pane  8
Falling Asleep  9
A Purification  10
A Dance  11
The Fear of Love  12
Seventeen Years  13
To What Listens  14
Woods  15
The Lilies  16
Forty Years  17
A Meeting  18
The Watchers  19
Another Descent  20
Below  21

## II

The Star  25
The Hidden Singer  26
The Necessity of Faith  27
To the Holy Spirit  28
Ripening  29
The Way of Pain  30

We Who Prayed and Wept    32
Grief    33
In Place of Happiness    34
Fall    35
A Grace    36
An Autumn Burning    37

## III

No Thanks    41
A Warning to My Readers    42
Walnut St., Oak St., Sycamore St., etc.    43
Creation Myth    44
Now    46
The Mad Farmer March    47
Confession    48
The First    49
Walking on the River Ice    50
The Necessity of Flight    51
Throwing Away the Mail    52
Except    53
Eight Below    54
For the Future    55
An Encore Maybe    56
Traveling at Home    57

## IV

Ronsard's Lament for the
Cutting of the Forest of Gastine    61
The Salad    63
Watching the Mid-Autumn Moon    68

## V Three Kentucky River Poems

July, 1773    71
1975    80
The Slip    83

## VI Horses

Horses    87

I

# Stay Home

I will wait here in the fields
to see how well the rain
brings on the grass.
In the labor of the fields
longer than a man's life
I am at home. Don't come with me.
You stay home too.

I will be standing in the woods
where the old trees
move only with the wind
and then with gravity.
In the stillness of the trees
I am at home. Don't come with me.
You stay home too.

# To Gary Snyder

After we saw the wild ducks
and walked away, drawing out
the quiet that had held us,
in wonder of them and of ourselves,
Den said, "I wish Mr. Snyder
had been here." And I said, "Yes."
But it cannot be often as it was
when we heard geese in the air
and ran out of the house to see them
wavering in long lines, high,
southward, out of sight.
By division we speak, out of wonder.

# For the Hog Killing

Let them stand still for the bullet, and stare the
    shooter in the eye,
let them die while the sound of the shot is in the
    air, let them die as they fall,
let the jugular blood spring hot to the knife, let
    its freshet be full,
let this day begin again the change of hogs into
    people, not the other way around,
for today we celebrate again our lives' wedding with
    the world,
for by our hunger, by this provisioning, we renew
    the bond.

# Goods

It's the immemorial feelings
I like the best: hunger, thirst,
their satisfaction; work-weariness,
earned rest; the falling again
from loneliness to love;
the green growth the mind takes
from the pastures in March;
the gayety in the stride
of a good team of Belgian mares
that seems to shudder from me
through all my ancestry.

# The Adze

I came out to the barn lot
near nightfall, past supper time,
where he stood at work still
with the adze, that had to be
finely used or it would wound
the user—a lean old man
whose passion was to know
what a man could do in a day
and how a tool empowered the hand.
He paused to warn: stay back
from what innocence made dangerous.
I stayed back, and he went on
with what he had to do
while dark fell round him.

# The Cold Pane

Between the living world
and the world of death
is a clear, cold pane;
a man who looks too close
must fog it with his breath,
or hold his breath too long.

# Falling Asleep

Raindrops on the tin roof.
What do they say?
We have all
    been here before.

# A Purification

At start of spring I open a trench
in the ground. I put into it
the winter's accumulation of paper,
pages I do not want to read
again, useless words, fragments,
errors. And I put into it
the contents of the outhouse:
light of the sun, growth of the ground,
finished with one of their journeys.
To the sky, to the wind, then,
and to the faithful trees, I confess
my sins: that I have not been happy
enough, considering my good luck;
have listened to too much noise;
have been inattentive to wonders;
have lusted after praise.
And then upon the gathered refuse
of mind and body, I close the trench,
folding shut again the dark,
the deathless earth. Beneath that seal
the old escapes into the new.

# A Dance

The stepping stones, once
in a row along the slope,
have drifted out of line,
pushed by frosts and rains.
Walking is no longer thoughtless
over them, but alert as dancing,
as tense and poised, to step
short, and long, and then
longer, right, and then left.
At the winter's end, I dance
the history of weather.

# The Fear of Love

I come to the fear of love
as I have often come,
to what must be desired
and to what must be done.

Only love can quiet the fear
of love, and only love can save
from diminishment the love
that we must lose to have.

We stand as in an open field,
blossom, leaf, and stem,
rooted and shaken in our day
heads nodding in the wind.

# Seventeen Years

They are here again,
the locusts I baited my lines with
in the summer we married.
The light is filled
with the song the ground exhales
once in seventeen years.
And we are here with the wear
and the knowledge of those years,
understanding the song
of locusts no better than then,
knowing the future no more than they
who give themselves so long
to the dark. What can we say,
who grow older in love?
Marriage is not made
but in dark time, in the rhymes,
the returns of song,
that mark time's losses.
They open our eyes
to the dark, and we marry again.

5/29/74

# To What Listens

I come to it again
and again, the thought of the wren
opening his song here
to no human ear—
no woman to look up,
no man to turn his head.
The farm will sink then
from all we have done and said.
Beauty will lie, fold
on fold, upon it. Foreseeing
it so, I cannot withhold
love. But from the height
and distance of foresight,
how well I like it
as it is! The river shining,
the bare trees on the bank,
the house set snug
as a stone in the hill's flank,
the pasture behind it green.
Its songs and loves throb
in my head till like the wren
I sing—to what listens—again.

# Woods

I part the out thrusting branches
and come in beneath
the blessed and the blessing trees.
Though I am silent
there is singing around me.
Though I am dark
there is vision around me.
Though I am heavy
there is flight around me.

# The Lilies

Hunting them, a man must sweat, bear
the whine of a mosquito in his ear,
grow thirsty, tired, despair perhaps
of ever finding them, walk a long way.
He must give himself over to chance,
for they live beyond prediction.
He must give himself over to patience,
for they live beyond will. He must be led
along the hill as by a prayer.
If he finds them anywhere, he will find
a few, paired on their stalks,
at ease in the air as souls in bliss.
I found them here at first without hunting,
by grace, as all beauties are first found.
I have hunted and not found them here.
Found, unfound, they breathe their light
into the mind, year after year.

# Forty Years

Life is your privilege, not your belonging.
It is the loss of it, now, that you will be singing.

# A Meeting

In a dream I meet
my dead friend. He has,
I know, gone long and far,
and yet he is the same
for the dead are changeless.
They grow no older.
It is I who have changed,
grown strange to what I was.
Yet I, the changed one,
ask: "How you been?"
He grins and looks at me.
"I been eating peaches
off some mighty fine trees."

# The Watchers

The horses graze the winter slope
and then go to the high ground
and stand, watching the traffic
along the road, the slow river,
the trees leaning and straightening
in the wind. The day's time
is their time. They do not move
toward it or away. Their minds
are at home in this world,
diminished by no question.

# Another Descent

Through the weeks of deep snow
we walked above the ground
on fallen sky, as though we did
not come of root and leaf, as though
we had only air and weather
for our difficult home.
                        But now
as March warms, and the rivulets
run like birdsong on the slopes,
and the branches of light sing in the hills,
slowly we return to earth.

# Below

Above trees and rooftops
is the range of symbols:
banner, cross, and star;
air war, the mode of those
who live by symbols; the pure
abstraction of travel by air.
Here a spire holds up
an angel with trump and wings;
he's in *his* element.
Another lifts a hand
with forefinger pointing up
to admonish that all's not here.
All's not. But I aspire
downward. Flyers embrace
the air, and I'm a man
who needs something to hug.
All my dawns cross the horizon
and rise, from underfoot.
What I stand for
is what I stand on.

II

# The Star

Flying at night, above the clouds, all earthmarks spurned,
lost in Heaven, where peaceful entry must be earned,
I have no pleasure here, nothing to desire.
And then I see one light below there like a star.

# The Hidden Singer

The gods are less
for their love of praise.
Above and below them all
is a spirit that needs
nothing but its own
wholeness,
its health and ours.
It has made all things
by dividing itself.
It will be whole again.
To its joy we come
together—the seer
and the seen, the eater
and the eaten, the lover
and the loved.
In our joining it knows
itself. It is with us then,
not as the gods
whose names crest
in unearthly fire,
but as a little bird
hidden in the leaves
who sings quietly
and waits
and sings.

# The Necessity of Faith

True harvests no mere intent may reap.
Finally we must lie down to sleep
And leave the world, all we desire
To darkness, malevolence, and fire.
Who wakes and stands his shadow's mark
Has passed by mercy through the dark.
We save the good, lovely, and bright
By will in part, in part delight;
But they live through the night by grace
That no intention can efface.

# To the Holy Spirit

O Thou, far off and here, whole and broken,
Who in necessity and in bounty wait,
Whose truth is light and dark, mute though spoken,
By Thy wide grace show me Thy narrow gate.

# Ripening

The longer we are together
the larger death grows around us.
How many we know by now
who are dead! We, who were young,
now count the cost of having been.
And yet as we know the dead
we grow familiar with the world.
We, who were young and loved each other
ignorantly, now come to know
each other in love, married
by what we have done, as much
as by what we intend. Our hair
turns white with our ripening
as though to fly away in some
coming wind, bearing the seed
of what we know. It was bitter to learn
that we come to death as we come
to love, bitter to face
the just and solving welcome
that death prepares. But that is bitter
only to the ignorant, who pray
it will not happen. Having come
the bitter way to better prayer, we have
the sweetness of ripening. How sweet
to know you by the signs of this world!

# The Way of Pain

1.
For parents, the only way
is hard. We who give life
give pain. There is no help.
Yet we who give pain
give love; by pain we learn
the extremity of love.

2.
I read of Abraham's sacrifice
the Voice required of him,
so that he led to the altar
and the knife his only son.
The beloved life was spared
that time, but not the pain.
It was the pain that was required.

3.
I read of Christ crucified,
the only begotten Son
sacrificed to flesh and time
and all our woe. He died
and rose, but who does not tremble
for his pain, his loneliness,
and the darkness of the sixth hour?
Unless we grieve like Mary
at His grave, giving Him up
as lost, no Easter morning comes.

4.

And then I slept, and dreamed
the life of my only son
was required of me, and I
must bring him to the edge
of pain, not knowing why.
I woke, and yet that pain
was true. It brought his life
to the full in me. I bore him
suffering, with love like the sun,
too bright, unsparing, whole.

# We Who Prayed and Wept

We who prayed and wept
for liberty from kings
and the yoke of liberty
accept the tyranny of things
we do not need.
In plenitude too free,
We have become adept
beneath the yoke of greed.

Those who will not learn
in plenty to keep their place
must learn it by their need
when they have had their way
and the fields spurn their seed.
We have failed Thy grace.
Lord, I flinch and pray,
send Thy necessity.

# Grief

The morning comes. The old woman, a spot
of soot where she has touched her cheek, tears
on her face, builds a fire, sets water to boil,
puts the skillet on. The man in his middle years,
bent by the work he has done toward the work
he will do, weeps as he eats, bread in his mouth,
tears on his face. They shape the day for its passing
as if absent from it—for what needs care, caring,
feeding what must be fed. To keep them, there are only
the household's remembered ways, etched thin
and brittle by their tears. It is a sharp light
that lights the day now. It seems to shine,
beyond eyesight, also in another day
where the dead have risen and are walking
away, their backs forever turned. What
look is in their eyes? What do they say
as they walk into the fall and flow of light?
It seems that they must know where they are going.
And the living must go with them, not knowing,
a little way. And the dead go on, not turning,
knowing, but not saying. And the living
turn back to their day, their grieving and staying.

# In Place of Happiness

In happiness, we reject the fair
Fields and groves of Paradise,
And so by grief are driven there;
Where pleasures fail, pains suffice.

# Fall

*for Wallace Fowlie*

The wild cherries ripen, black and fat,
Paradisal fruits that taste of no man's sweat.

Reach up, pull down the laden branch, and eat;
When you have learned their bitterness, they taste sweet.

# A Grace

*for Gregory Bateson*

I

The storied leaves fall through the stories
of air. Their call is to return. The ground
gathers them all into its plot, as it gathers
fallen hands. Autumnal as stories begin,
they end when their patterns rhyme, in beauty, vernal.

II

In rhyme of hand with leaf, time with time,
we recall what grief forgets, what joy has never
seen: the chief beauty of the world,
pattern of patterns. Though deaf, we dance. The music
that moves us, deaf and blind, is our relief.

# An Autumn Burning

*for Kenneth Rexroth*

In my line of paperwork
I have words to burn: leaves
of fallen information, wasted
words of my own. I know a light
that hastens on the dark
some work deserves—which God forgive
as we must hope. I start the blaze
and observe the fire's superlative
hunger for literature. It touches pages
like a connoisseur, turns them.
None can endure. After the passing
of that light, there is sunlight
on the ash, in the distance singing
of crickets and of birds. I turn,
unburdened, to life beyond words.

III

# No Thanks

Shadows rise out of the hollows,
draw across the hills.
A fading radiance is in the sky.
Tired, I hear my thoughts speak
in buxom syllables
of song sparrow and bobwhite.
A breeze moves the highest
oak leaves over the barn.
A day in my life is ending
well, no thanks to many
who would claim the credit.

# A Warning to My Readers

Do not think me gentle
because I speak in praise
of gentleness, or elegant
because I honor the grace
that keeps this world. I am
a man crude as any,
gross of speech, intolerant,
stubborn, angry, full
of fits and furies. That I
may have spoken well
at times, is not natural.
A wonder is what it is.

# Walnut St., Oak St.,
# Sycamore St., etc.

So this is what happened
to the names of the trees!
I heard them fly up,
whistling, out of the woods.
But I did not know
where they had gone.

# Creation Myth

This is a story handed down.
It is about the old days when Bill
and Florence and a lot of their kin
lived in the little tin-roofed house
beside the woods, below the hill.
Mornings, they went up the hill
to work, Florence to the house,
the men and boys to the field.
Evenings, they all came home again.
There would be talk then and laughter
and taking of ease around the porch
while the summer night closed.
But one night, McKinley, Bill's young brother,
stayed away late, and it was dark
when he started down the hill.
Not a star shone, not a window.
What he was going down into was
the dark, only his footsteps sounding
to prove he trod the ground. And Bill
who had got up to cool himself,
thinking and smoking, leaning on
the jamb of the open front door,
heard McKinley coming down,
and heard his steps beat faster
as he came, for McKinley felt the pasture's
darkness joined to all the rest
of darkness everywhere. It touched

the depths of woods and sky and grave.
In that huge dark, things that usually
stayed put might get around, as fish
in pond or slue get loose in flood.
Oh, things could be coming close
that never had come close before.
He missed the house and went on down
and crossed the draw and pounded on
where the pasture widened on the other side,
lost then for sure. Propped in the door,
Bill heard him circling, a dark star
in the dark, breathing hard, his feet
blind on the little reality
that was left. Amused, Bill smoked
his smoke, and listened. He knew where
McKinley was, though McKinley didn't.
Bill smiled in the darkness to himself,
and let McKinley run until his steps
approached something really to fear:
the quarry pool. Bill quit his pipe
then, opened the screen, and stepped out,
barefoot, on the warm boards. "McKinley!"
he said, and laid the field out clear
under McKinley's feet, and placed
the map of it in his head.

# Now

I used to wish for a breakthrough.
Now I worry about what into.

# The Mad Farmer March

Instead of reading Chairman Mao
I think I'll go and milk my cow.

# Confession

I wish I was easy in my mind, but I ain't.
If it wasn't for anger, lust, and pride, I'd be a saint.

# The First

The first man who whistled
thought he had a wren in his mouth.
He went around all day
with his lips puckered,
afraid to swallow.

# Walking on the River Ice

A man could be a god
if the ice wouldn't melt
and he could stand the cold.

# The Necessity of Flight

How light the burdens of despair!
I hang on to hope, my whole
Weight swinging in the air,
The only respite: a little
Moment, now and then, of flight.

# Throwing Away the Mail

Nothing is simple,
not even simplification.
Thus, throwing away
the mail, I exchange
the complexity of duty
for the simplicity of guilt.

# Except

Now that you have gone
and I am alone and quiet,
my contentment would be
complete, if I did not wish
you were here so I could say,
"How good it is, Tanya,
to be alone and quiet."

# Eight Below

Eight below zero on the fifth of March!
Maybe the world is coming to an end.
Well, good riddance, anyhow, to part of it.

# For the Future

Planting trees early in spring,
we make a place for birds to sing
in time to come. How do we know?
They are singing here now.
There is no other guarantee
that singing will ever be.

# An Encore Maybe

To see this little one find the door
to this world, enter, draw breath,
struggle upright from the floor,
nuzzle, find the tit, and suck,
you would think it had been born before.

# Traveling at Home

Even in a country you know by heart
it's hard to go the same way twice.
The life of the going changes.
The chances change and make a new way.
Any tree or stone or bird
Can be the bud of a new direction. The
natural correction is to make intent
of accident. To get back before dark
is the art of going.

IV

# Ronsard's Lament for the Cutting of the Forest of Gastine

Old forest, tall household of the birds, no more
Will nimble deer browse as they did before
Deep in your peaceful shade, and your green mane
No more will gentle summer's sun and rain.
No more will the amorous shepherd come to sit
Against a tree, his sheepdog at his feet,
To play upon his four-holed flute in praise
Of pretty Janet and her pleasing ways.
All will be mute, Echo be still for good.
There will be a field where your great trees stood,
Their airy shadows shifting in the light. Now
You will feel the coulter and the plow.
Your deep silence gone, breathless with fear,
Satyr and Pan will not again come here.
Farewell, old hall of the wind's high harmony,
Where I first made my lyre's tongues agree;
Where Calliope, so beautiful and good,
Gave me the love of her great sisterhood,
As if she cast a hundred roses over me;
Where Euterpe at her own breast nourished me.
Farewell, old trees, farewell, high sacred heads,
Once honored with rites and flowers, holy deeds,
Disdained by travelers now, your death their plight
Who burn in the summer sky's naked light—
Who, knowing no more your fresh green shade,
Curse your destroyers, wishing them destroyed.
Farewell, old oaks, once honored by our creed

As fellow citizens, Dodonean seed,
Jupiter's trees, that first gave food to men,
Ungrateful men, who did not understand
Beneficence—a people utterly gross
To massacre these fathers who nourished us.
The man who trusts this world will not be free
Of grief. How true, O gods, is that philosophy
Which says that all things in the end will perish,
That by the deaths of forms new forms will flourish.
In time, a peak in Tempe's Vale will stand,
And Mount Athos will be a bottomland;
Neptune's fields, in time, will stand in grain.
All forms will pass, matter alone remain.

*(Elegy XXIV, starting with line 27, deleting lines 43 and 44.)*

# The Salad

*(Pierre de Ronsard: La Salade)*

Wash your hands, get them good and clean,
Hurry and find a basket, friend Jamyn;
Let us gather a salad, and so unite
To our passing lives this season's fruit.
With a straying foot, a roving eye,
Here, there, in a hundred out-of-the-way
Places, at the top of a bank, across a narrow
Ditch, or in a field left fallow
That of itself, never disturbed
By the plow, bears every kind of herb —
I'll go this inviting way alone.
And you, Jamyn, take that direction.
For the tufted shepherd's purse look carefully,
And for the narrow-leafed daisy;
Watch for burnet, good for the circulation
And for the spleen and for indigestion.
I will gather wife-of-the-moss, the sweet
Rampion with its tuberous root,
The buds of currants, fresh opening,
Whose green is first to announce the Spring.
Then, reading the ingenious Ovid,
The splendid verses where he is Love's guide,
Step by step, still rambling, let us go
Back home. Rolling our sleeves to the elbow,
We'll wash our greens handful by handful
In the sacred waters of my beautiful
Fountain, blanch them in salt water, stir

And sprinkle them with red wine vinegar,
Richen them with the good oil of Provence.
Oil that comes from the olive trees of France
Ruins the stomach, it is so inferior.

    And so, Jamyn, you know my sovereign cure
Until I rid my veins forever
Of this abominable quartan fever
That has so used me up, body and mind,
So weakened me that I may never mend.
You'll say this fever has set my senses loose,
That I've gone mad—with my salad and my Muse.
And you'll be right. I want it to be so,
Because this madness rectifies my woe.

    And then you'll tell me it is best to live
Like those parasites sweating so to thrive
On Kings, on credit and good luck,
Bloated on pomp and honor that they suck.
I know it all, too well; want none of it,
For such a life makes life a counterfeit.
It requires one to lie, deceive, and flatter;
Believe, admire in mask; laugh without laughter.
No more for me. I want no part of it.
To live that life makes life a counterfeit.
To follow in your steps at court, I grow
Too sick, too deaf, too sluggish, too slow,
Too much afraid; besides, I now require
A restful quietude, no public care
Hung over my poor forehead like a sword.

    In a little while all courtiers will be bored,
Failed, gray—or dead, lying in a coffin.
In this one present that God has given

They will have spoiled their natural gentility
To hold too close this world's prosperity —
Uncertain good, and usually gone
Before it reaches the third generation.
For Fortune with her unsettled disposition
Cannot for long abide such men's ambition,
Demonstrating by their sudden fall
That it's a thing of wind, this free-for-all
Of a world; and the man is lost indeed
Who lives exiled at court, nor dies in bed
At home. Spare me the pomp and privilege
That gull us with appearance, sacrilege
Of guile — that wear and fret a man inside
With gnawing envy, care, and pride.

The man who climbs to honor in trivial matters
Seems a Colossus held in fetters,
Confined by hasps and hinges, bars and nails;
His face is puffed with rage; he rails
Like Neptune — or if he dared he would.
His marvelous swelling astounds the neighborhood,
Rich outwardly with azure and with gold,
But when we look inside this blazoned, bold
Corpse, there's only plaster, kneaded clay.
The imposture's laid bare then — all false display!
And henceforth this Colossal trash
From his high eminence can abash
Only the simplest fool; those with good sense
Grin in contempt at such a performance.

Ignorant man, so short of wits and days,
Forgets that it is only a game Death plays,
A game of chess, this brief and painful life;

And that when Death has pacified its strife
He mixes all together in his sack
Knight, Pawn, King, Queen, Rook.
And thus the earth beneath the same verdure
Holds commoners and kings, by law of Nature
Who without prejudice, impartial mother,
Cares no more for one than for the other.
And thus she demonstrates that worldly glory
And greatness make a sounding, hollow story.

   Ah, but Virgil pleases when he sings
The old father of Corycia who each spring,
Busy with his hoe through daylight's length,
Worked his meagre fields with all his strength,
And coming home at evening bought no wine
Or any costly bread or meat in town,
But spread his frugal table with things to eat
That to his healthy hunger seemed more sweet,
Better and tastier than any Lord's
Who, stuffed with meat and honor, bored,
Picks and finicks over earth's largess
That eaten without savour is savourless.
Which do you think was happiest of these two:
That great Crassus, to his 'position' true,
Who, envious of Pompey's Triumph, of that *word,*
Went out to die by the Parthian sword,
Or this old husbandman who stayed at home,
Lived in his garden, and never set foot in Rome?

   If we only knew, said Hesiod, how well
Our need is served by the asphodel,
And how to care for it, the human soul
Would prosper, and the half surpass the whole.

By the half he meant the plain coherent life
Of country people, free of ambition's grief,
Who have the health of unpretentious things;
By the whole he meant the happiness of kings.
Nature, said the good Horace,
Is content with little, and our human race
Does not need much; yet we are so beguiled
That for the whole we let the half be spoiled.

    Let's gather our salad before I preach all day!
It's too cold out for a sick man, you say?
What of it! You be the doctor, Jamyn, my friend,
But let me live at ease until the end
At least, and don't waste your breath
By prophesying either life or death;
For you no more than I should think of ways
To shorten, much less to lengthen out my days.
It is necessary to board old Charon's bark
At last, that tomb vaulted like the ark.
Birth is the fatal passage, and here is why:
If he weren't born, no man would ever die.
And he's a fool who hopes for a better sum;
Birth and death are the same, the two are one.

Notes
*The poet* Amadis Jamyn *was first Ronsard's page and then his secretary.* M. Licinius Crassus, *after the war against the pirates, received an 'ovation;' his colleague and rival,* Pompey, *was granted a 'triumph,' a higher honor. In order to increase his military standing,* Crassus *undertook a campaign against the Parthians, during which he was killed.*

# Watching the Mid-Autumn Moon

Young, we had not enough
respect for the changing moon.
Then the days seemed to pass
only to return again.
Now, having learned by loss
that men's days part from them
forever, we eat and drink
together beneath the full moon,
acknowledging and celebrating
the power that has bereft us
and yet sheds over the earth
a light that is beautiful.

*After the painting and poem by Shen Chou.*

68

# Three Kentucky River Poems     V

# July, 1773

Seventeen seventy one
and two. In those years the fame
of the Long Hunters passed back
through the settlements, with news
of a rich and delightful country
to the west, on the waters of the Ohio.
My father and uncles held council
over their future prospects.
In the vigor of manhood and full
of enterprise, they longed to see
for themselves. They could not remain
confined in the sterile mountains
of Virginia, where only small parcels
of fertile land could be found
at any one place. As soldiers
of the Indian Wars, each had
from the governor a grant
of four hundred acres, which had only
to be located and surveyed.

                        And so,
having first planted their corn
about the tenth of May
in the year 1773, they set out
to visit this land of promise,
five of them, taking along
Sam Adams, a neighbor's son,

nineteen years of age.
They sought their future homes,
their fortunes, and the honor
of being among the first
in that western wilderness.

They reached the Great Kanahway,
then known as New River,
about the middle of May.
Having sent back their horses,
they selected suitable trees,
felled them, hollowed the trunks,
and so made two canoes
to carry them and their baggage:
rifles, ammunition, tomahawks,
butcher knives, blankets,
fishing tackle, and gigs.
And then, after their rough
overland passage on horseback,
how lightly and quietly they passed
over the surface of the water,
their prows breaking the reflections
of the trees in the early morning.

They entered the Ohio on
the first of June, the opening
of light on that wide water,
its stillnesses and solitudes.
Opposite the mouth of the Sciota
they saw an old French town

of nineteen or twenty houses,
hewed logs and clapboard roofs,
vacant and deserted, small
and silent among the great trees.

On June thirteenth, a Sunday,
they were met by the bearer of a letter
"to the gentlemen settlers"
from Richard Butler, a white man
who had lived at Chilicothe
with the Shawanoes several years:
"They claim an absolute rite
to all that country that you
are about to settle. It does not
lie in the power of those
who sold it to give this land.
Show a friendly countenance
to your present neighbors, the Shawanoes.
It lies in your power to have
good neighbors or bad, as they
are a people very capable
of discerning between good treatment
and ill. They expect you
to be friendly with them,
and to endeavor to restrain
the hunters from destroying the game."
And this they took to show
the means by which an All-wise
Providence opened the way
for exploration and settlement.

They camped on July fourth
at Big Bone Lick.
"It was a wonder to see
the large bones that lies there
which has been of several
large big creatures."
They used the short joints
of the backbones for stools,
and the ribs for tent poles
to stretch their blankets on.
Here they met a Delaware
about seventy years old.
Did he know anything
about these bones? He replied
that when he was a boy "they
were just so as you now see them."
And so they had come to a place
of mystery; they could not
enter except in awe.

At daylight on the morning
of July eighth, they reached
the mouth of the Kentucky River,
which they called the Lewvisa.
This was the foretold stream
that would carry them southward
into the heart of promise.
They set against its current,
reaching by nightfall the mouth
of a stream they called Eagle Creek

for the eagles they saw hovering
there, in the evening light.

And the next day went on
to the mouth of what is now
Drennon Creek, where the river
was nearly closed by a stone bar,
and there they left their boats.
They crossed a bottomland
through a forest of beech trees,
gray trunks in the shade
of gold-green foliage,
and after a mile came to
"a salt lick which was
a wonder to see—a mile
in length and one hundred yards
in breadth, & the roads that came
to that lick no man would believe
who did not see, & the woods
around that place were trod
for many miles, that there
was not as much food
as would feed one sheep."

They encountered there great numbers
of buffalo, elk, deer,
beaver, wolves, and bears.
The commotion of the herds was astonishing,
their tramplings and outcries,
the flies and the dust. There

where the salts of the ground flowed
to the light, the living blood
of that country gathered, throve
in its seasonal pulse—such
a gathering of beasts as these men
had never seen. Through the nights
they heard them, dreamed them,
seeming to comprehend them
more clearly in dream
than in eyesight, for that upwelling
and abounding, unbidden by any
man, was powerful, bright,
and brief for men like these,
as a holy vision. Waking,
they could not keep it. They did not.

Five days and six
nights they camped there,
examining the lick, killing
game, making several
surveys of land. The uplands
around the lick they found
"very good, mostly
oak timber; a great many
small creeks and branches;
scarce as much water
among them all as would
save a man's life
while he traveled across them."

One day, engaged in this work,
Uncle James and his neighbor's
son, Sam Adams, were passing
round the outskirts of the lick,
where had gathered a large herd
of the buffalo. The beasts
pressed together for the salt,
stomped, coughed, suckled
their calves, the dust rising
over their humps and horns,
their tails busy at flies.
They minded less than flies
the two men who moved
around them, thinking of other
lives, times to come.
And yet Sam Adams, boylike
perhaps, though he was nineteen
and a man in other ways,
would be diverted from his work
to gaze at the buffalo,
more numerous than all
his forefathers' cattle, oblivious
abundance, there by no man's
will—godly, he might
have thought it, had he not
thought God a man.

                    And why
he shot into the herd

is a question he did not answer,
anyhow until afterwards,
if at all—if he asked at all.
He saw an amplitude
so far beyond his need
he could not imagine it,
and could not let it be.
He shot.

And the herd, unskilled
in fear of such a weapon
or such a creature, ran
in clumsy terror directly
toward the spot where the boy
and the man were standing.
Agile, the boy sprang
into a leaning mulberry.
Not so young, or active,
or so used to haste,
Uncle James took shelter
behind a young hickory
whose girth was barely larger
than his own.

Then it seemed
the earth itself rose,
gathered, fled past them.
The great fall of hooves shook
ground and tree. Leaves
trembled in the one sound.
Dust hid everything

from everything. Bodies
beat against each other
in heavy flight. Black horns
sheared bark from the hickory
that protected Uncle James.

It fled. The hectic pulse
died in the ground. The dust
thinned. Day returned,
as it seemed, after nightmare.
And there was Sam Adams
looking out of his tree
at Uncle James, who looked
back, his hat now tilted.
"My good boy, you must not
venture that again."

And they walked southeast from there
two days, some thirty miles,
left a tomahawk and fish gig
at a fine spring, and marked
a gum sapling at that place.

*(This poem makes extensive borrowings from various accounts of
the McAfee brothers' 1773 expedition into Kentucky.)*

# 1975

Another rainy winter,
the third one in a row.
Cattle stand in mud.
Fog rises in rain.
The old river, maker
of the hills, runs muddy,
swollen, day after day.
All here is shaped by search,
water finding its way.

The valley keeps the shape
of the escape of water.
Moving water carved it
in violence so long and slow
it was gentle. It hollowed
the long main stem
of the valley, drew its fingers
down the tributaries and coves,
and did it all in little
displacements of stone, little
shifts and slips, nudgings,
wedgings of frozen soil,
meltings. And all the while
the forest stood unmoved
on the slopes, canebrake
grew to the water's edge,

speckled bass soared
in pools clear as the sky.

Millions of years it worked
at this great work, missing
nothing, meticulous and patient
as a colony of ants. It worked
like a mind, a godly fathering
and mothering mind, teaching
its creature how to grow.

In flood it bore the humus
of the forest floor, and left it
on the bottomlands downstream,
richness to make myth
behind us, so great it was,
so soon destroyed.

It was old light the currents bore,
old time itself, the past
more vital and complete
than myth or memory, laid down
to bless the fields. And then
we cut the trees, opened
the mountainsides for coal,
cast the mountains down
into the valleys, and so destroyed
the ancient light of the ground,
time gone into the power
to come again. That history

is the undoing of light,
days turned against days.
The river has become the gut
of greed. Human evil
moves in its currents now,
each rise a kind of weapon,
the old clarity gone.

# The Slip

*for Donald Davie*

The river takes the land, and leaves nothing.
Where the great slip gave way in the bank
and an acre disappeared, all human plans
dissolve. An aweful clarification occurs
where a place was. Its memory breaks
from what is known now, begins to drift.
Where cattle grazed and trees stood, emptiness
widens the air for birdflight, wind, and rain.
As before the beginning, nothing is there.
Human wrong is in the cause, human
ruin in the effect—but no matter;
all will be lost, no matter the reason.
Nothing, having arrived, will stay.
The earth, even, is like a flower, so soon
passeth it away. And yet this nothing
is the seed of all—the clear eye
of Heaven, where all the worlds appear.
Where the imperfect has departed, the perfect
begins its struggle to return. The good gift
begins again its descent. The maker moves
in the unmade, stirring the water until
it clouds, dark beneath the surface,
stirring and darkening the soul until pain
perceives new possibility. There is nothing
to do but learn and wait, return to work
on what remains. Seed will sprout in the scar.
Though death is in the healing, it will heal.

Horses VI

# Horses

When I was a boy here,
traveling the fields for pleasure,
the farms were worked with teams.
As late as then a teamster
was thought an accomplished man,
his art an essential discipline.
A boy learned it by delight
as he learned to use
his body, following the example
of men. The reins of a team
were put into my hands
when I thought the work was play.
And in the corrective gaze
of men now dead I learned
to flesh my will in power
great enough to kill me
should I let it turn.
I learned the other tongue
by which men spoke to beasts
— all its terms and tones.
And by the time I learned,
new ways had changed the time.

The tractors came. The horses
stood in the fields, keepsakes,
grew old, and died. Or were sold
as dogmeat. Our minds received

the revolution of engines, our will
stretched toward the numb endurance
of metal. And that old speech
by which we magnified
our flesh in other flesh
fell dead in our mouths.
The songs of the world died
in our ears as we went within
the uproar of the long syllable
of the motors. Our intent entered
the world as combustion.
Like our travels, our workdays
burned upon the world,
lifting its inwards up
in fire. Veiled in that power
our minds gave up the endless
cycle of growth and decay
and took the unreturning way,
the breathless distance of iron.

But that work, empowered by burning
the world's body, showed us
finally the world's limits
and our own. We had then
the life of a candle, no longer
the ever-returning song
among the grassblades and the leaves.

Did I never forget?
Or did I, after years,
remember? To hear that song

again, though brokenly
in the distances of memory,
is coming home. I came to
a farm, some of it unreachable
by machines, as some of the world
will always be. And so
I came to a team, a pair
of mares—sorrels, with white
tails and manes, beautiful!—
to keep my sloping fields.
Going behind them, the reins
tight over their backs as they stepped
their long strides, revived
again on my tongue the cries
of dead men in the living
fields. Now every move
answers what is still.
This work of love rhymes
living and dead. A dance
is what this plodding is.
A song, whatever is said.

Design by David Bullen
Typeset in Mergenthaler Sabon
by Robert Sibley
Printed by McNaughton-Gunn
on acid-free paper